PIERRE BERTON

# REVENGE OF THE TRIBES

ILLUSTRATIONS BY HENRY VAN DER LINDE

An M&S Paperback Original from
McClelland & Stewart Inc.
*The Canadian Publishers*

An M&S Paperback Original from McClelland & Stewart Inc.

First printing September 1991

Copyright © 1991 by Pierre Berton Enterprises Ltd.

---

**Canadian Cataloguing in Publication Data**

Berton, Pierre, 1920–
  Revenge of the tribes

(Adventures in Canadian history. The battles of the War of 1812)
"An M&S paperback original".
Includes index.
ISBN 0-7710-1429-5

1. Canada – History – War of 1812 – Participation,
Indian – Juvenile literature.* 2. United States –
History – War of 1812 – Participation, Indian –
Juvenile literature. 3. Canada – History – War of
1812 – Indians – Juvenile literature.* 4. United
States – History – War of 1812 – Indians – Juvenile
literature. 5. Indians of North America – Canada –
Juvenile literature. 6. Indians of North America –
Northwest, Old – Juvenile literature. I. Van der
Linde, Henry. II. Title. III. Series: Berton,
Pierre, 1920–   . Adventures in Canadian history.
The battles of the War of 1812.

FC442.B48 1991    j971.03′4′08997    C91-094455-5
E359.85.B48 1991

---

Cover design by Tania Craan
Text design by Martin Gould
Cover illustration by Scott Cameron
Interior illustrations by Henry Van Der Linde
Maps by James Loates
Editor: Peter Carver

Typesetting by Pickwick

Printed and bound in Canada

McClelland & Stewart Inc.
*The Canadian Publishers*
481 University Avenue
Toronto, Ontario
M5G 2E9

# CONTENTS

Overview: The peculiar war     9

1 The Shawnee brothers     20

2 Scorching the earth     30

3 A hunger for glory     40

4 A strange weariness     49

5 The Battle of Frenchtown     56

6 Massacre     69

7 The captive     79

Index     87

Maps appear on pages 34 and 58-9

*Private in the 49th Regiment of Foot, garrisoned at York, 1812*

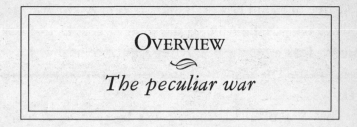

OVERVIEW

*The peculiar war*

W HEN WAR BROKE out between the United States and
Canada in June of 1812, John Richardson rushed to
join the colours. He was only fifteen – a slight, curly-
headed, clean shaven youth – but, unlike so many of his
neighbours, he was eager to serve his country.

Many of his neighbours on the Detroit river were recent
arrivals from the United States, reluctant to fight their
former compatriots. But Richardson came of solid Canadian stock. His mother's father, John Askin, was a famous
fur trader. His grandmother was an Ottawa Indian of the
Algonquin nation. And so young John, to his considerable
delight, found himself accepted as a "gentleman volunteer"
in a regular regiment – the British 41st – stationed in Fort
Amherstburg not far from the present site of Windsor. In
the next thirty months, he probably saw more of the War
of 1812 than any other teenager in Upper Canada.

After fifteen months of fighting, Richardson was captured by the Americans – a capture that tells us a good deal
about that most peculiar of wars. Unlike so many prisoners

in so many jail cells around the world, he could be fairly sure of decent treatment by his enemies, because he knew so many of them. His grandfather, John Askin, had only to write a note to the American colonel at Fort Detroit asking him to look after the boy. After all, the colonel was Askin's son-in-law. The man in charge of his prison was another relative.

The War of 1812, then, must be seen as a civil war fought by men and women on both sides of a border that all had ignored until hostilities broke out. Many were former neighbours who spoke the same language and were often related to one another. Unlike the Richardsons, three out of every five were former Americans.

Some had come up from the United States after the American Revolution. These "Tories", as their compatriots called them, were fiercely loyal to the British Crown. Canadians know them as "United Empire Loyalists." They formed the backbone of the volunteer civilian army, known as the militia.

The others were more recent arrivals. They came to Canada because the land was cheap and taxes almost non-existent. They wanted to be left alone to clear the land of stumps, to drain the marshes, till the soil, and harvest their crops of wheat, barley and corn, or tend the apple, pear and cherry trees that grew so abundantly along the border.

For them, life was hard enough without war. They built their own cabins and barns with the help of their neighbours and, since there was scarcely anything resembling a shop or a store, they made everything themselves, from farm implements to the homespun clothing that was the universal dress. Those villages that existed at all were mere huddles of shacks. Communication was difficult and sometimes impossible. Newspapers were virtually unknown. In the single room schoolhouses, children learned to read, write, and figure – not much more.

These people didn't want to fight any more than their counterparts, the civilian soldiers south of the border. It was indeed a peculiar war that moved along in fits and starts, like a springless buggy bumping over a dirt track. At harvest time and seeding, farmers on both sides deserted or were sent off to tend to their crops. In winter, nothing moved; it was too cold to fight, and so each autumn all activity was postponed until spring.

It was, like so many conflicts, a very silly war. Communication was so bad that hundreds of soldiers, not to mention generals, had no idea it had begun. The last bloody battle was fought long after peace had been declared. The problems that had caused the war in the first place – Great Britain's attacks on American shipping – were solved well before the war ended. But the war went on – men were maimed and killed, farms were vandalized, barns were burned, whole communities put to the torch, and "traitors" hanged for no purpose.

Why were young Canadians like John Richardson fighting young Americans along the international border? The Canadians who fought did so to protect their country from attack. The Americans were fighting for something less tangible – their honour. Once again, they felt, the British were pushing them around. The War of 1812 was in many ways a continuation of the War of Independence fought forty years before.

It started with Napoleon Bonaparte, the dictator of France. Bonaparte wanted to conquer all of Europe, and so the British found themselves locked in a long and bloody struggle with him – a struggle that began with the great British naval victory at Trafalgar and ended a decade later with the famous battle of Waterloo.

But in their zeal to conquer Napoleon, the British pushed the Americans too far. By boarding American ships on the high seas and kidnapping American sailors for service in the Royal Navy – on the grounds that these seamen were actually British deserters – they got the Americans' backs up. Then, in order to strangle the French by a sea blockade, the British announced they would seize any ship that dared sail directly for a French port. By 1812, they had captured four hundred American vessels, some within sight of the U.S. coast.

That was too much. The United States at last declared war on Great Britain. Since it couldn't attack England directly, it determined to give the British a bloody nose by invading its colony, Canada.

To former President Thomas Jefferson, that seemed "a mere matter of marching." Surely the United States, with a population of eight million, could easily defeat a mere three hundred thousand Canadians!

The odds, however, weren't quite as unequal as Jefferson supposed. Great Britain had 17,000 regular troops stationed in Upper and Lower Canada. The entire U.S. regular army numbered only 7,000, many of them badly trained.

Moreover, the British controlled the water routes – Lakes Huron, Erie and Ontario, and also the St. Lawrence River. For that was the key to both mobility and communication. The roads were almost worthless when they existed at all – not much more than rutted cart tracks. Everything – supplies, troops and weapons – moved by water.

When the war broke out, the Americans were prevented from using this water highway by the presence of the Royal Navy on the lakes. A British express canoe could move swiftly and fearlessly all the way to Lake Superior, carrying dispatches. But the American high command had difficulty communicating at all, which explains why its outposts didn't know for a month that the war was on. The Americans had to use express riders – bold men on horseback, plunging through a jungle of forest and swamp and exposed at every turn to an Indian ambush.

No wonder, then, that almost from the outset the War of 1812 developed into a shipbuilding contest, with both sides feverishly hammering men-of-war to completion in a race to control the lakes.

The Indians were another asset for the British. The

Americans had turned them into enemies, burning their crops and villages and hunting them down like wild animals. In American eyes, the Indians were an obstruction to be pushed aside or eliminated as the pioneers and settlers moved resolutely westward. But the Canadians hadn't fought the Indians since the days of the French-English wars fifty years before. They saw them as harvesters of fur, or, as in the case of the Mohawks of the Grand Valley, loyal subjects of the King.

The American attitude caused John Richardson's boyhood friend, Tecumseh, to move into Upper Canada from the U.S. with his followers to fight on the British side. The native allies numbered no more than 2,000 in all, but with their woodcraft they made a formidable enemy. The Americans were terrified of the Indians. The mere hint that a force of natives was advancing could send a chill through the blood of the citizen soldiers of Ohio or Kentucky.

As a member of the regular army, John Richardson wore a scarlet uniform and carried a musket almost as tall as himself. This awkward, muzzle-loading "Brown Bess" was the basic infantry weapon – and a notoriously inaccurate one. The little one-ounce (.03 kg) ball, wobbling down the smooth barrel, could fly off in any direction. Richardson and his fellow soldiers didn't bother to aim their weapons; they pointed them in the direction of the enemy, waited for the command, and then fired in unison.

The effect of several hundred men, marching in line and in step, shoulders touching, and advancing behind a spray of lead, could be devastating. The noise alone was terrifying. The musket's roar makes the crack of a modern rifle sound like a popgun. Smokeless powder was unknown; after the first volley the battlefield was shrouded in a thick fog of grey.

It required twelve separate movements to load and fire a musket. A well-drilled soldier could get off two or three shots a minute. By that time he was usually close enough to the enemy to rely on his bayonet.

Young Richardson learned to remove a paper cartridge from his pouch, tear off the top with his teeth, pour a little powder in the firing pan and the rest down the barrel. Then he stuffed it with wadding, tapped it tight with his ramrod and dropped in the ball. When he pulled the trigger it engaged the flintlock whose spark (he hoped) would ignite the powder in the pan and send a flash through a pinhole, exploding the charge in the barrel. As Richardson himself discovered at the Battle of Frenchtown later that year, it didn't always work. The phrase "a flash in the pan" comes down to us from those days.

Some of the American woodsmen used the famous Tennessee rifle, a far more accurate weapon because of the spiral groove inside the barrel. That put a spin on the ball – in the same way a pitcher does in baseball – making it far easier to hit the target. However, it was slower to load and was used mainly by snipers or individual soldiers.

A more terrible weapon was the cannon, which operated on the same flintlock principle as the musket. From the

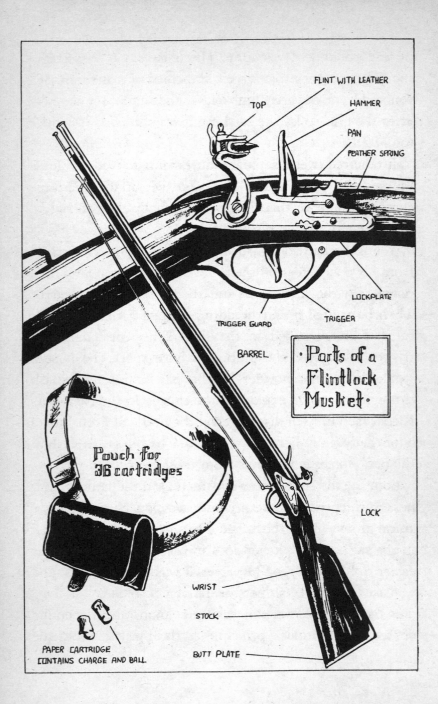

FLINT WITH LEATHER

TOP

HAMMER

PAN

FEATHER SPRING

LOCKPLATE

TRIGGER

TRIGGER GUARD

BARREL

Parts of a Flintlock Musket

Pouch for 36 cartridges

LOCK

WRIST

STOCK

PAPER CARTRIDGE CONTAINS CHARGE AND BALL

BUTT PLATE

tiny three-pounders (1.4 kg) to the big twenty-four-pounders (11 kg), these weapons were identified by the weight of shot they hurled at the ramparts of the defenders. A sixteen-pound (7 kg) ball of solid pig iron (known as "roundshot") could knock down a file of two dozen men. Bombs – hollowed out shot, crammed with powder and bric-à-brac, and fused to explode in mid-air – were even more devastating. Every soldier feared the canister and grape shot – sacks or metal canisters filled with musket balls that broke apart in the air, sending scores of projectiles whirling above the enemy.

Crude as they seem to us now, these weapons caused a dreadful havoc for the soldiers who fought in the war. Men with mangled limbs and jagged wounds faced searing pain because anaesthetics had not been invented. Yet, grievously wounded men pleaded with army surgeons to amputate a wounded limb as quickly as possible for fear of gangrene. They swallowed a tot of rum or whisky, held a bullet ("biting the bullet") between their gritted teeth, and endured fearful agony as the knives and saws did their work.

Sanitation in the field was primitive, for science had not yet discovered that diseases were caused by germs. Measles, typhus, typhoid, influenza, and dysentery probably put more men out of action than the enemy. The universal remedy was liquor – a daily glass of strong Jamaica rum for the British, a quarter pint (0.2 L) of raw whisky for the Americans. In battle after battle, the combatants on both sides were at least half drunk. Hundreds of youths who had never touched hard liquor in their lives learned to stiffen their resolve through alcohol in the War of 1812.

These were civilian soldiers, members of the militia. In Canada, the Sedentary Militia, largely untrained, was available in times of crisis. Every fit male between 18 and 60 was required to serve in it when needed. Few had uniforms, and those who did were as tattered as beggars. Often they were sent home to their farms after a battle to be called up later.

Some signed up in the Incorporated Militia of Upper Canada for the duration of the war. These were young men inspired by patriotism, a sense of adventure, or the bounty of 80 dollars paid to every volunteer upon enlistment. In Lower Canada, a similar body of the Select Embodied Militia, composed of men between 18 and 25, was drawn by lot to serve for a minimum of two years. They were paid and trained as regular soldiers. In addition some regular units were also recruited in Canada, bearing such names as The Glengarry Fencibles or the Canadian Voltigeurs.

The American draftees and volunteers were engaged by the various states for shorter periods – as little as a month, as much as a year. Most refused to serve beyond that period; few were properly trained. Born of revolution and dedicated to absolute democracy, the United States had decided against a large standing army. The citizen soldiers even elected their own officers – an awkward and not very efficient process, sneered at by the regulars. And they were recruited to fight *only* in defence of their country.

That caused a major problem for the United States. Legally, the state militia didn't have to cross the border. Hundreds who had been drafted reluctantly used that excuse when their superiors tried to goad them into attacking Canada. Jefferson had said it was "a mere matter of marching," but when the armies reached the border, the marching stopped.

They didn't want to fight any more than their former compatriots, now tilling the fields and tending the orchards on the other side. That was one of the reasons why this peculiar war ended in stalemate. The Americans derived very little benefit from it; nor did the Indians, who were eventually betrayed by both sides when the peace talks were held. The only real victors were the Canadians, who got no territory but gained something less tangible, yet in the end more precious. Having helped to hurl back five American armies, the plain people who had once been so indifferent to the war developed both a sense of pride and a sense of community. They had come through the fire and they had survived. In a very real sense the War of 1812 marked the first faint stirrings of a united Canadian nation.

# CHAPTER ONE

## The Shawnee brothers

THIS IS A STORY of revenge and retaliation. It is the story of how a force of white men led by a future president of the United States savagely attacked and destroyed an Indian village. It is the story of how, in the war that followed, the Indians claimed a terrible price from the American soldiers sent to hunt them down.

Although they received precious little credit for it, the Indians played a key role in defeating the American armies who tried to invade Canada in 1812 and 1813. Indeed, it's possible that without the Indians' help, the British and Canadians who took credit for winning the war might have lost it. For that, the country owed a great deal to the remarkable Shawnee war chief, Tecumseh, whose hatred of the Americans caused him to side with the British.

Tecumseh's relentless enemy was William Henry Harrison, the ambitious governor of the Indiana territory south of Lake Michigan. Harrison wanted to swallow three million acres (1.2 million hectares) of native hunting grounds that had never been given up by the Indians. For that he had the official agreement of the President himself, James Madison.

In 1809 Harrison got it – or thought he did – for a pittance. At a mere two dollars an acre, it cost him only about fifty thousand dollars; it was worth six million. In short it was a barefaced steal. Harrison had the agreement of the major tribes – Miami, Delaware, Eel and Potawatomi. But he forgot the Shawnee. They were thought of as intruders, having been driven north from their original hunting grounds in Kentucky. Ignoring them was Harrison's mistake.

Into Harrison's capital of Vincennes in August of 1810 rode Tecumseh with a delegation of warriors to bargain with the governor. The meeting was to be held at his estate in the shade of a canopy not far from Harrison's great brick mansion. Here were assembled the town's leading citizens, guarded by a platoon of soldiers, all craning their necks to see the Shawnee chief who had the impertinence to keep their governor waiting for several days. Now, at last he arrived, accompanied by thirty warriors, their faces smeared with vermilion paint, and all armed with tomahawks and clubs.

The Americans saw a handsome figure, tall for his tribe – at least five foot ten (1.75 m) – with an oval rather than an angular face, his complexion light copper, his nose handsome and straight. Everyone who met him noticed his eyes, which were clear, bright hazel under dark brows, and his teeth, which were white and even.

He was naked to the waist, his head shaved save for a scalp lock. He walked with a brisk, elastic step in spite of a bent leg fractured and poorly set after a youthful fall from a pony. There were some who thought him the finest specimen of a man they had ever seen, but no authentic likeness exists on paper or canvas because he refused to have his portrait painted by a white man.

He would not join the white delegation, seated under the canopy. He intended to speak as in a council circle, which puts every man on the same level. "Houses" he said, "are made for white men to hold councils in. Indians hold theirs in the open air."

"Your father requests you sit by his side," said Harrison's interpreter.

Tecumseh raised an arm and pointed to the sky.

"My father! The Great Spirit is my father! The earth is my mother – and on her bosom I will recline."

Such was the man that the frustrated Harrison was forced to deal with in his attempt to seize the Indian hunting grounds. When the Shawnee chief spoke, the Governor had to listen – for this half-naked man in the deerskin leggings was one of the greatest orators of his time. His reputation had preceded him. He was known as a supreme performer who could rouse his audience to tears, laughter, fury, and action. Even those who couldn't understand his words were said to be held by the power of his voice.

As the council proceeded, Tecumseh made it quite clear that he intended to prevent the land sold by the other tribes from falling into the hands of the whites. Harrison had no choice but to stop the surveys. He knew now that he would never get his land at two dollars per acre until the power of Tecumseh and his mysterious brother, known as The Prophet, was broken forever.

The two didn't look like brothers. Tecumseh was almost too handsome to be true. His younger brother, however, was ugly, awkward, and one-eyed. The Prophet was elusive and unpredictable. Tecumseh was a clear-eyed military genius. Yet the two were a team, their personalities and philosophies interlocking like pieces of a jigsaw puzzle.

Unlike the Prophet, Tecumseh was a warrior – but a warrior of a different breed. The ritual tortures that were part of the culture of many tribes sickened him. He did not believe that it made a man braver to eat the heart of a bold but defeated enemy. He would not allow his followers to kill or rape women and children – a practice that had until recently been normal in many European armies.

Tecumseh dreamed the ancient dream of an Indian confederacy stretching from Florida to Lake Erie – an alliance strong enough to resist white pressure. To achieve that end, he was prepared to travel astonishing distances preaching to the various tribes. Already the nucleus of a new alliance was forming at the junction of the Tippecanoe river and the Wabash. More than a thousand members of half a dozen tribes had flocked there in answer to the call of Tecumseh's brother. The settlement was known as Prophet's Town.

*Tecumseh and The Prophet*

Harrison felt the time was ripe for a preventive war. He wanted to smash the power of the Shawnee brothers, put his surveyors back on the Indian hunting grounds, and head off an Indian alliance with the British to the north.

He chose to launch the military campaign in August of 1811. Tecumseh was in the south rallying the tribes. Harrison meant to attack and destroy Prophet's Town before the Shawnee war chief returned.

Tecumseh had already warned his brother that he must not, on any account, be prodded into battle. But Harrison meant to prod him. He marched to the edge of the disputed territories, built a fort (which was named "Fort Harrison"), and then invaded the Indian territory at the head of a thousand men.

On November 6, about a dozen miles (20 km) from his objective, he drew up his forces in battle order. A delegation of Indians arrived on a peace mission. Harrison assured them that all he sought was a proper camping ground. They agreed to meet and talk the following day; but there was no meeting.

We don't know what the Indians were thinking because the only accounts of the battle come from white men. But some things are fairly certain. The Indians didn't trust Harrison; they expected him to attack and were determined to attack first. In that they were correct. But the battle, when it came, was started by accident. A nervous sentry fired his weapon at an unseen enemy, and chaos followed.

Harrison was pulling on his boots at four the following morning when he heard yells and gunfire. The struggle that followed was bitter. Harrison escaped being killed only because his grey horse went missing and he was forced to mount a different one. The Indians failed to recognize it and instead shot one of his colonels, mounted on a similar horse.

But they could not overcome a superior force, including 250 well-trained soldiers from the 4th U.S. infantry. Harrison rode from point to point trying to control the battle. The Indians were acting in a most un-Indian fashion, responding with considerable discipline to signals made by the rattling of deer horns. They would fire a volley, then retreat out of range, reload and advance again.

By daybreak the entire line of soldiers was engaged. As the Indians began to falter at last, Harrison determined on a charge from the flanks. That was the climax of the battle. The level of the sound became unbearable – an ear-splitting mixture of savage yells, shrieks of despair, the roar of musketry, agonizing screams, victorious shouts, and dying cries mingling in a continuous terrifying uproar that would ring in the ears of survivors long after the last wound was healed.

Harrison's charge succeeded. Out of ammunition and arrows, the Indians retired across the marshy prairie where horses could not follow. The Americans uttered prayers of thanks, bound up their wounds, scalped all the dead Indians and killed one who was wounded – for white soldiers could be just as savage as the so-called "savages".

Two days later they swept through Prophet's Town – empty save for one aged squaw – on a mission of revenge and plunder. They destroyed everything, including all the beans and corn that they themselves could not eat – some three thousand bushels (110,000 L) stored for the winter. They found British weapons in some of the houses, which confirmed their suspicion that British agents had been encouraging the Indians to attack. Then they burned all the houses and sheds and left. Thus ended the Battle of Tippecanoe, which has sometimes been called the first battle in the War of 1812.

More than any other incident, it was this vicious attack on a peaceful Indian community that helped create the horror that followed. For the Indians the land was sacred; in their view, nobody owned it; the hunting grounds were open to all. But now they were being swindled of their birthright; and that swindle was achieved by bloodshed and brutality. In the events that followed one might well ask: who were the real savages – the Indians fighting for their heritage, or Harrison and his soldiers intent on taking it by force?

The battle was celebrated as a great victory for Harrison who eventually used Tippecanoe as a rallying cry in his successful attempt to win the U.S. presidency in 1840. But he lost almost one-fifth of his force and he failed to break

*Tecumseh and William Henry Harrison meet at Vincennes:*
*"My father! The Great Spirit is my father!"*

up Tecumseh's confederacy or diminish the Prophet's power.

The raids on the white settlements continued. Settlers and soldiers were ambushed. Whole families were scalped and mutilated by tribesmen driven into a rage by Harrison's attack. Farmers were forced to abandon their fields and cabins. Some fled the territory.

Tecumseh returned at last to Prophet's Town and later he spoke of his experience: "I stood upon the ashes of my own home, where my own wigwam had sent up its fire to the Great Spirit, and there I summoned the spirits of the braves who had fallen in their vain attempts to protect their homes from the grasping invader, and as I snuffed up the smell of their blood from the ground I swore once more eternal hatred – the hatred of an avenger."

Harrison's boast that he had shattered the alliance was hollow. By May of 1812, Tecumseh had six hundred men under his command making bows and arrows. In Washington, war fever rose, fueled by tales of frontier violence and the legend of Tippecanoe. Tecumseh waited and held his men back for the right moment. For a while he would pretend to be neutral, but when the moment came he was determined to lead the forces of his confederacy across the border to fight beside the British against the common enemy.

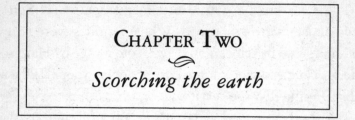

# CHAPTER TWO
## Scorching the earth

ON JUNE 18, 1812, when the Americans declared war against Great Britain, Governor Harrison's folly in making an enemy of Tecumseh became apparent. On both sides of the border, the various tribes flocked to support the British and the Canadians.

It was Tecumseh at the head of his own braves who helped the British win the first battle, seizing Fort Detroit and most of Michigan Territory. (See *The Capture of Detroit*, Book #1 in this series.)

Later, at a battle at Queenston Heights, the British were again victorious, again helped by the Indians, this time the Mohawks under William Norton. (See *The Death of Isaac Brock*, Book #2 in this series.)

With Detroit in ruins, with hundreds of Americans now held prisoner, and the British controlling both sides of the northern border, the United States made plans for another expedition. Governor Harrison was called into service to lead an army of Kentuckians to regain Detroit for the United States.

*American troops sweep through and destroy Prophet's Town on a mission of revenge and plunder.*

Every able-bodied man in Kentucky seemed to want to fight. By the end of the year, more than eleven thousand Kentuckians were in the army. In many ways they were like their traditional enemies, the Indians. They were hardy, adventurous men, romantic, touchy, proud, bold, courageous, and often very cruel. The state of Kentucky itself lay on the old Indian frontier. Memories remained of bloody Indian wars. Youths were raised on tales of British and Indian raiders killing, scalping, and ravaging during the Revolution (though killing and scalping wasn't confined to one side). The Battle of Tippecanoe had revived the fear and hatred. The reports of British weapons found at Prophet's Town confirmed to the people of the state that John Bull – as they called the British – was again behind the Indian troubles.

Harrison, newly appointed Commander-in-Chief of the Army of the Northwest, received the dreadful news of the fall of Detroit on August 26, two days before he reached Cincinnati. He had twenty-one hundred men under his command and an equal number on their way to join his force.

He faced a monumental task. He was short of almost everything – food, clothing, equipment, weapons, ammunition, flint, and swords. The only gun was an ancient cast-iron four-pounder (1.8 kg). Autumn was fast approaching with its chilling rain and sleet. He would have to hack new roads through forest and swamp, and build blockhouses and magazines. And all the time he would be watched and harassed by the Indians.

He was determined to crush all Indian resistance without mercy. Columns of cavalry fanned out to destroy every Indian village within sixty miles (100 km). Some of these excursions cost the Americans dearly. One officer, Colonel John Scott, insisted on leading an attack on Elkheart River in Indiana Territory even though his fellow officers urged him not to go. Scott mounted his horse, crying out, "As long as I am able to mount you, none but myself shall lead my regiment. . . . " That was the death of him. Exhausted after a march of three days and nights, he was barely able to return to camp, and shortly after he died.

Harrison's policy was to search and destroy. He saw no difference between neutral and hostile tribes. His intention was to the turn the frontier country into a no man's land, denying both shelter and food to the Indians. Mounted troops burned several hundred houses, ravaged the cornfields, destroyed crops of beans, pumpkins, potatoes, and melons, ransacked the graves and scattered the bones. The Potawatomi and Miami fled to the British for protection and waited for revenge.

Harrison planned to move his army to the foot of the rapids of the Maumee in three columns. One force on his left would march from the recently built Fort Winchester along the route of the Maumee River. The central force of twelve hundred would follow the road to the same rendez-

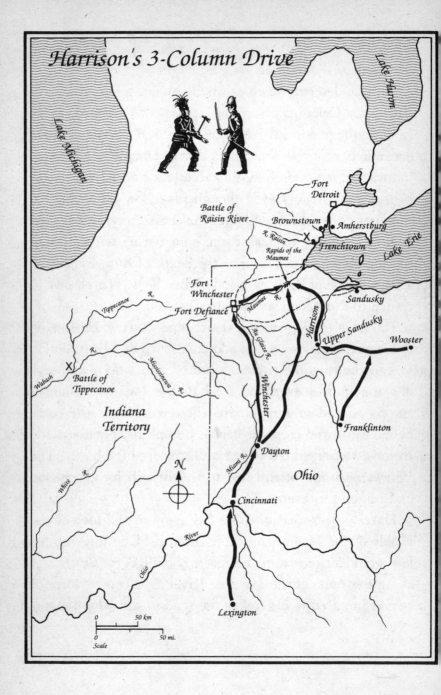

# Harrison's 3-Column Drive

Lake Huron

Lake Michigan

Fort Detroit

Battle of
Raisin River

Brownstown

Amherstburg

R. Raisin

Frenchtown

Lake Erie

Rapids of the
Maumee

Fort
Winchester

Fort Defiance

Maumee R.

Sandusky

Au Glaize R.

Harrison

Upper Sandusky

Wooster

Tippecanoe R.

R.

Mississinewa R.

Winchester

Wabash R.

X Battle of
Tippecanoe

Franklinton

Indiana
Territory

White R.

Miami R.

Dayton

Ohio

N

Cincinnati

River

Ohio

Lexington

0        50 km
0            50 mi.
Scale

vous. A division on their right would proceed to Wooster, Ohio, by way of the Upper Sandusky River.

But one force was soon pinned down on the Maumee because the promised supplies were not forthcoming. A second mounted brigade was ordered to dash to the foot of the rapids of the Maumee to harvest several hundred hectares of corn for the famished troops. But the scalping of a ranger less than two hundred yards (180 m) from the camp caused such a panic that the mission had to be abandoned. Rations remained scarce, in spite of Harrison's promises. There was little flour, almost no salt, and the beef – what there was of it – was deplorable.

Ignoring strict orders, the men wandered out of camp, wasting their ammunition in search of game. Many were barefoot, their clothes in rags. They slept on frozen ground, some without blankets. More than two hundred were sick at one time. By November they began to die from typhus.

And Detroit, as well as most of Michigan Territory, was still in British hands.

Harrison's fellow governor, Isaac Shelby of Kentucky, was determined to retake Detroit before winter, and therefore ordered more attacks on the Indians. Two thousand mounted volunteers, enlisted for only thirty days, were ordered to march against the tribes in both Indiana and Illinois territories. Shelby believed he could succeed if the weather remained dry. But if it rained, he would be stuck at the Rapids of the Maumee until the lake was sufficiently frozen to bear the weight of the army and its baggage.

Then came appalling news from the Niagara frontier. A second American army had tried to invade Canada at Queenston and had been hurled back from the heights by a combined force of British regulars, Canadian volunteers, and Mohawk Indians. Coming on the heels of the disaster at Detroit, this was a major blow to American morale.

By October 22, Harrison found he could not set a firm date for the recapture of Detroit. He would need a million rations at the Rapids of the Maumee before he could mount an attack. But the driving rain that everyone feared now came. The roads were in desperate condition. The horses, attempting to struggle through the swamps, were dying by the hundreds. He couldn't move his supplies or his guns.

With his left flank wide open to Indian attack, Harrison decided to prevent further Indian raids by striking at the Miami villages along the Mississinewa, a tributary of the Wabash. On November 25 Lieutenant-Colonel John Campbell and six hundred cavalry and infantry set out to do the job. The results were disastrous.

In spite of Campbell's attempts at secrecy, the Miamis knew of the plan ahead of time. They left their villages, waited until the troops were exhausted, and then launched a night attack, destroying a hundred horses, killing eight men, and wounding forty-eight.

A false rumour spread, that the dreaded Tecumseh was on his way at the head of a large force. Campbell's dejected band beat a hasty retreat. His men were now in a bad way.

The weather turned bitterly cold. Their food was almost gone. The wounded were dying from gangrene. The remainder suffered from frostbite. A relief party finally got them into Greenville where it was found that three hundred men – half of Campbell's force – were disabled. Harrison had lost the core of his cavalry while the Indians had escaped untouched.

Meanwhile his left column, under General James Winchester, was still pinned down near the junction of the Maumee and the Au Glaize River waiting for supplies. It was impossible to get them through the Black Swamp that lay between the Sandusky and the Maumee. The troops were out of flour, existing on bad beef, pork, and hickory nuts. Sickness and death had reduced the force to eleven hundred. Winchester's forces numbered eighteen hundred at the beginning of October. Daily funerals cast a pall over the camps. The growing realization that there was no chance of invading Canada that year contributed to the loss of morale.

On Christmas Day, Winchester got orders to move to the rapids as soon as he received two days' rations. There he would be joined by the right wing of the army. Two days later the supplies arrived and on December 29 the troops set off for the rapids. Few armies have presented such a ragtag appearance. In spite of the midwinter weather, scarcely one man possessed a greatcoat or cloak. Only a lucky few had woollen garments. The remainder were dressed in the clothes they wore when they left Kentucky, their cotton shirts torn, patched, and ragged, hanging to their knees, their trousers also cotton. Their matted hair fell uncombed over their cheeks. Their slouch hats had long since been worn bare. Those who owned blankets wrapped them about their bodies as protection from the blizzards, holding them in place by broad belts of leather into which were jammed axes and knives. The officers were scarcely distinguishable from the men. They carried swords or rifles instead of long guns, and daggers in place of knives.

Now these men were forced to become beasts of burden because the horses were not fit to pull the weight. Harnessed five to a sleigh, they hauled their equipment through snow and water for eleven days. The sleighs were badly made – too light to carry the loads, not large enough to cross the half-frozen streams. Provisions and men were soon soaked through. The days were bad but the nights were a horror. Knee-deep snow had to be cleared away before a camp could be made. Fire had to be struck from flint on steel. The wet wood often refused to burn. It was so cold they couldn't prepare beds for themselves. The Kentuckians simply toppled down on piles of brush before the smoky fires and slept in their steaming garments.

Then, on the third day, a frantic message from Harrison arrived: *turn back!* The General had picked up another rumour that the formidable Tecumseh and several hundred Indians were in the area. With the Indians at his rear and with no certainty of provisions at the rapids, any further movement towards Canada this winter would be foolhardy.

But Winchester was in no mood to retreat. He was a man who had suddenly been released from three months of dreadful frustration. Now at last he was on the move. It must have seemed to him like some sort of progress. It was action of a kind and at the end, who knew? More action, even glory, beckoned. He had no stomach to turn in his tracks and return to "that loathsome place", nor did his men. And so they moved on to tragedy.

# CHAPTER THREE

## A hunger for glory

AS WINCHESTER'S FORCES staggered on toward the Rapids of the Maumee, ignoring Harrison's warning, Lieutenant-Colonel Henry Procter at Fort Amherstburg, across the river from the captured Detroit, came to the wrong conclusion. He was convinced that the Americans had gone into winter quarters. His Indian spies had observed no movement around the Winchester camp for several weeks. He was convinced that Harrison had decided to hold up any attempt to recapture Detroit till spring. That was just as well, because Procter had only a skeleton force of soldiers and a handful of Indians to fight the Americans.

The Indians concerned him. He couldn't control them. He really didn't like them. Although they fought on the British side, their loyalty wasn't really to the British or to the Americans but to their own kind. They would support the British, but only as long as they believed it suited their own purposes.

From the British point of view the Indians didn't observe the so-called rules of warfare, which were, of course, white European rules. Tecumseh was the only chief who could restrain his followers from killing and torturing prisoners and ravaging women and children. But Tecumseh had headed south to try to draw the Creek and the Choctaws to his confederacy, and his brother, the Prophet, had returned to the Wabash.

Procter needed to keep the Indians active. He had attempted to capture Fort Wayne, but that attempt failed though it slowed Harrison's advance. Now he was under orders from the higher-ups to avoid all offensive warfare. His only task was to defend against the invader.

He had to be careful. The Indians' loyalty depended on a show of British resolution. The only way their confidence and good will could be preserved was to attack the Americans and kill as many as possible and let the braves have their way with the rest.

Thus his strategy was to let the Americans keep the tribes in a fury – which was what they were doing. Harrison's attempt to subdue the Indians of the northwestern frontier had delayed his advance until midwinter and caused widespread anger among the various bands. Some six thousand had been left homeless, nineteen villages had been ravaged, seven hundred lodges burned, thousands of litres of corn destroyed.

Savagery increased on both sides. The Kentuckians took scalps whenever they could. Nor were women and children safe from the army. In one unprovoked attack on an Indian village near Mansfield south of Lake Erie, the Ohio militiamen had burned all the houses and shot several of the inhabitants.

The worst attacks the previous fall had been against the Indian villages on the Peoria lakes southwest of Lake Michigan. These were destroyed by a force of American rangers and volunteers under Governor Ninian Edwards of Illinois Territory. One raid would not soon be forgotten. A mounted party under a captain named Judy came upon an Indian couple on the open prairie. When the man tried to surrender, Judy shot him through the body. Chanting his death song, the Indian killed one of Judy's men and was in turn riddled with bullets. A little later the same group captured and killed a starving Indian child.

In their rage, Edwards' followers scalped and mutilated the bodies of the fallen, and ransacked the Indian graves for plunder. Small wonder, then, that the Potawatomi chief, Black Bird, cried out in fury to a Canadian: "The way they treat our killed and remains of those that are in their graves to the west make our people mad when they meet the Big Knives. Whenever they get any of our people into their hands they cut them like meat into small pieces."

All that fall the Indians continued to concern Procter. They devoured his provisions at an alarming rate and Tecumseh's restraining hand was absent. Procter solved part of his supply problem by sending most of the Indians to the Rapids of the Maumee where several hundred hectares of corn were waiting to be harvested – the same corn that Harrison had been trying to seize.

Harrison's scorched earth policy backfired – to the gain of the British. Indian spies infiltrated Ohio and reported that Winchester was again advancing. The British sent couriers to the villages of the Ottawa and the Potawatomi in Michigan Territory and to the Miami in Indiana. Within a month the native force had increased from three hundred to almost eight hundred braves, all stirred to a fever by Harrison's army.

On January 11, Winchester's army reached the Rapids of the Maumee. Two days later Procter got the news and quickly called out the militia and assembled the Indians.

Procter planned to ravage the Detroit frontier in order to deny the Americans provisions and shelter. On January 14, he sent Major Ebenezer Reynolds of the Essex militia with two companies and a band of Potawatomis to the little village of Frenchtown on the River Raisin. Reynolds' orders were to destroy the village and all its supplies and to remove the French-speaking settlers to Canadian soil.

That would not be a pleasant task. Nobody wanted his home destroyed, his property removed, or his cattle driven off and killed by Indians. The settlers had worked hard to improve their farms, which lay on both sides of the narrow low-banked river. Their town, a simple row of some twenty houses, squatted on the north bank three miles (5 km) from the mouth. It was not designed as a fort. Its only protection was a fence of split pickets to secure the yards and gardens.

The villagers were in a panic. As Reynolds and his men moved in, a delegation slipped away heading for the Rapids of the Maumee to plead with Winchester for help. They carried a note for Harrison informing him that "five hundred true and brave Americans can secure the District of Erie – A timely approach of our armies will secure us from being forced to prison and the whole place from being burned by savage fury."

Winchester knew that if he was to save this settlement he must act at once. On January 17 he and his senior offi-

cers sat in council. Should they go to the relief of French-town? For almost four days word had been coming back of Indian outrages and British high-handedness.

Everything was being moved from the village – cattle, sleighs, grain, and foodstuffs. Winchester's information was that the British force was ridiculously small. But it was building rapidly. If the Americans moved quickly they could acquire food for themselves at Frenchtown by taking three thousand barrels of flour and much grain. That prospect must have seemed as tempting as the relief of the villagers.

*General James Winchester's Kentuckian soldiers slog through the muck of the River Maumee prior to their move to Frenchtown.*

Lieutenant-Colonel John Allen rose. He was a graceful, commanding presence, perhaps the most popular man in Winchester's army and certainly the most distinguished and most eloquent. A handsome Kentuckian, tall, sandy-haired, blue-eyed, he was one of the state's great orators – a leading lawyer, a state senator, and once a candidate for governor. When he spoke all would listen because he commanded as much respect as, if not more than, his general.

He was fed up with inactivity – weary of slow movements that got him nowhere. He hungered for action and now he saw his chance. The army could go to the aid of the defenceless inhabitants of Frenchtown, obtain the desperately needed food at the settlement, and strike a decisive blow against the British. That would open the road to Detroit some thirty miles (50 km) to the northwest. At last they could cover themselves with glory.

The council didn't need much convincing, nor did Winchester. Why wait for Harrison who was sixty-five miles (105 km) away? A victory over the British – *any* victory – could make Winchester a national hero. His men were as eager to move as he. The term of the six-month volunteers would end in February and they had refused to re-enlist. All wanted one brief taste of glory before returning home.

They had just received a welcome shipment of woollen underwear. Their morale, reduced by long weeks of inactivity and hunger, had risen again. And there was *food* at Frenchtown! Winchester, who had already asked for more reinforcements, now sent a second letter to Harrison announcing his intention to send a force to relieve Frenchtown and hold it.

One of Harrison's many frustrations during this exhausting fall and winter had been the collapse of communications. His letter to Winchester urging him to abandon his march to the rapids came too late. Winchester's reply that he would move ahead anyway didn't reach him until the force was actually at its destination. It was carried by an eighteen-year-old Kentucky volunteer named Leslie Combs, who, with a single guide, crossed one hundred miles (160 km) of trackless forest through snow so deep that the two men dared not lie down for fear of suffocating and were forced to sleep standing up. Exhausted, ill, and starving, the two reached Fort McArthur on January 9. Two days later, Harrison, at Upper Sandusky, got Winchester's letter.

Five days went by during which time Harrison had no idea of Winchester's position or plans. Then, on the night of January 16, he learned that Winchester had reached the rapids and wanted reinforcements. Apparently he was contemplating an attack. That news alarmed Harrison. If it was in his power he would call Winchester off!

He set off at once for Lower Sandusky, travelling so swiftly that his aide's horse dropped dead of exhaustion. There he immediately dispatched a troop of artillery, guarded by three hundred infantrymen, to Winchester's aid. The camp at the rapids was only thirty-six miles (60 km) away; but the roads were choked with drifting snow, and the party moved slowly.

When, on January 18, he received confirmation of Winchester's plan to relieve Frenchtown, he was thoroughly alarmed. He ordered two more regiments to march to the rapids, and set off himself in a sleigh. Its slowness annoyed him. He seized his servant's horse, and rode on alone. Darkness fell. The horse stumbled into a frozen swamp. The ice gave way. Harrison managed to free himself and pushed on through the night on foot. But he was too late.

# Chapter Four

## A strange weariness

WHILE HARRISON WAS desperately trying to reach Winchester to prevent a disaster, Winchester had already ordered Lieutenant-Colonel William Lewis and 450 troops to attack the enemy at Frenchtown on the River Raisin. Off went Lewis with three days' provisions, followed a few hours later by a second force of one hundred Kentuckians under the eager Lieutenant-Colonel Allen.

The two forces met at Presqu'Isle, a French Canadian village on the south side of the Maumee, twenty miles (32 km) from the rapids, eighteen miles (29 km) from the Raisin. The soldiers were overwhelmed by their first contact with anything remotely resembling civilization. A young soldier, Elias Darnell, wrote in his journal that, "the sight of this village filled each heart with emotions of cheerfulness and joy, for we had nearly five months in the wilderness, exposed to every inconvenience, and excluded from everything that had the appearance of a civilized country."

The inhabitants poured out of their homes waving white flags and shouting greetings. The troops were in high spirits. They knew that some would be corpses by the next day, but with the eternal optimism of all soldiers each man clung to the conviction that he would survive. Nonetheless, those who could write home sent letters to wives, parents and friends.

Colonel James Price, commander of the Jessamine Blues, wrote to his wife, Susan, in Kentucky, about their son. "Teach my son the habits of industry. . . . industry leads to virtue. . . . not a day must be lost in teaching him how to work. . . . it may be possible I may fall in battle and my only boy must know that his father, next to God, loves his country, and is now risking his life in defending that country against a barbarous and cruel enemy. . . . pray for me that you may be with me once more."

The following morning, January 18, as the Kentucky soldiers marched along the frozen surface of Lake Erie toward their objective, they met refugees from Frenchtown. They wanted to know what kind of artillery the British troops had. "Two pieces large enough to kill a mouse" came the reply.

From Frenchtown came word that the British were waiting. Lewis formed his troops up on the ice. As they came in sight of the settlement the lone British howitzer opened up. "Fire away with your mouse cannon!" some of the men cried. Then as the long drum roll sounded the charge they crossed the slippery river, clambered up the bank, leaped over the village pickets and drove the British back toward the forest.

The battle raged from 3 p.m. to dark. When dusk fell, the British had been driven two miles (3 km) from the village, and the Americans were in firm control. Now the soldiers at both Frenchtown and the rapids felt they were unbeatable – that they could roll right on to Detroit, cross the river, and capture Amherstburg.

The troops on the Raisin were dangerously exposed. Yet their eagerness for battle was such that Winchester would have found it difficult to withdraw them even if he had wanted to. But Winchester did not want to. Caught up in the ecstasy of victory, seeing himself and his army as saviours of his country's honour, he took what troops he could spare – fewer than three hundred – and marched off to Frenchtown.

There was another force drawing him and his men toward the village – an attraction quite as powerful as the prospect of fame and glory. Frenchtown, at that moment, was close to paradise. Here on the vine-clad banks of *la Rivière au Raisin* was luxury: fresh apples, cider by the barrel, sugar, butter, whiskey, and more – houses with roofs, warm beds, hearth sides with crackling fires, and the soft presence of women.

When Winchester arrived late on the twentieth, Lewis' men had already sampled these delights. There was some vague talk of reinforcing their position but that was only talk. The men were weary from fighting, unruly from drink, and in no mood to take orders.

The village was surrounded on three sides by a palisade constructed of eight-foot (2.4 m) logs, split and sharpened at the ends. These pickets, which did not come all the way down to the river bank, enclosed a compact community of log and shingle houses, interspersed with orchards, gardens, barns, and outbuildings. The whole space formed a rectangle two hundred yards (180 m) along the river and three hundred yards (275 m) deep.

On the right of the village, down the river, lay an open meadow with a number of detached houses. There, Lieutenant-Colonel Samuel Wells encamped his regulars. Winchester didn't like that. He thought that the regulars would be better placed within the palisade, but Wells insisted, pointing out that the regular soldiers should *always* be on the right of the militia. Winchester didn't argue. Wells's men were exposed, but he expected to find a better campground on the following day.

Leaving Wells in charge of the main camp, the general and his staff, including his teen-aged son, took up quarters on the south side of the river in the home of Colonel Francis Navarre, a local trader. This was a handsome building, the logs covered with clapboard, the whole shaded by pear trees originally brought from Normandy. Winchester was given a spacious guest room at the front of the house warmed by a fireplace.

It was now Wells's turn to object. He believed the general and his officers should be as close as possible to the troops on the far side of the river in case of sudden attack.

But James Winchester had made up his mind. For twenty years as a wealthy plantation owner he had enjoyed the creature comforts of a relaxed life. For five months without complaint he had slept out exposed to the weather, enduring hardships with his troops, existing on dreadful food – when there was food at all – drinking sometimes stagnant water scooped out of wagon tracks. Later he would argue that there was no house in Frenchtown – that he would have had to move some of the wounded. But that was clearly false.

The general and his troops were overcome with fatigue. The sudden victory, the almost magical appearance of food, drink, warmth, and shelter – the stuff of their dreams for these past weeks – gave them a dream-like confidence. There was talk of moving the camp to a better position, and on the following day the general and some of his officers rode out to look over the ground. Nothing came of that. Apparently it didn't occur to them that it might be a good idea to put the river between themselves and the British.

Wells left camp that morning, claiming he had baggage to collect at the rapids. Winchester thought Wells had lost faith in him. He sent a note to Harrison saying he didn't believe any attack would take place for several days. He learned later that Harrison had arrived at the Maumee rapids and that reinforcements were on their way. That added to the general air of self-satisfaction.

It is a rule of war that from time to time even the best generals suffer from a common failing – a refusal to believe their own intelligence reports. Mental blinkers narrow their vision. They reject any evidence that fails to support the truth as they see it. Winchester seemed deaf to all suggestions that the British were massing for attack.

Navarre's son, Peter, had scouted along the mouth of the Detroit River and returned to report that the British, with a large body of Indians, would be at the Raisin some time after dark. But even after a second scout confirmed the story, Winchester remained deaf to the warnings. Later in the evening one of Lewis's ensigns learned from a tavern-keeper that he had been talking to two British officers about an impending attack. But Lewis did not take that report seriously.

Some of Winchester's field officers expected that a council would be called that night. But there was no word from the general. Although Winchester had issued vague orders about strengthening the camp, little had been done. Nor did he issue ammunition, stored at Navarre's house – even though Wells's troops were down to ten rounds per man.

It was bitterly cold. The snow lay deep. Nobody had the heart to send pickets out onto the road leading into the settlement. One soldier, twenty-one-year-old William Atherton, noticed that most of the men acted as if they were perfectly safe, some wandering about town until late into the night. Atherton himself felt little anxiety, though he had reason to believe the situation was perilous. He slept soundly until awakened by the cry, "To arms! to arms!", the thundering of cannon, the roar of muskets, and the discordant yells of the attacking Indians.

# CHAPTER FIVE
## The Battle of Frenchtown

A T AMHERSTBURG LONG PAST midnight on January 19, the young people of the town and the officers of the garrison had gathered to hold a ball to celebrate the birthday of Queen Charlotte, the wife of George III, the mad old King of England. Suddenly in Draper's tavern the music stopped and in walked Procter's deputy, Lieutenant-Colonel St. George, dressed for the field. His voice, long accustomed to command, drowned the chatter.

"My boys," said the Colonel, "you must prepare to dance to a different tune; the enemy is upon us and we are going to surprise them. We shall take the route about four in the morning, so get ready at once."

Procter had just learned of the British defeat at the Raisin. He realized the Americans were in an exposed position and their numbers not large. He determined to scrape up as many men as he could and counter-attack at once.

Procter planned swiftly. He sent a detachment to defend Detroit. He left Fort Amherstburg virtually defenceless, manned only by the sick and least effective members of the militia. The remainder – every possible man who could be called into service, including provincial seamen from the gunboats – were sent across the river. He counted 597 able men and more than five hundred Indians – Potawatomi displaced from their homes by Harrison, with bitter memories of Tippecanoe; Miami, victims of the recent attacks at Mississinewa; and the Wyandot, under Chief Roundhead, formerly of Brownstown.

The first detachment left immediately, dragging three three-pound (1.4 kg) cannon and three small howitzers on sleighs. Fifteen-year-old John Richardson was young enough to find the scene romantic – the troops moving in a thin line across the frozen river under cliffs of rugged ice, their weapons, polished to a high gloss, glittering in the winter sunlight.

The following day the rest of the force crossed the river, spent the night at Brownstown and prepared to move early in the morning. As darkness fell, John Richardson's favourite brother, Robert, aged just fourteen, a midshipman in the Provincial Marine, sneaked into camp. His father, an army surgeon, had given him strict orders to stay out of trouble on the Canadian side, but he longed to see action and joined one of the gun crews.

In the morning, Procter moved his force of one thousand to Rocky River, twelve miles (20 km) from Brownstown and six miles (10 km) from Frenchtown. Two hours before dawn on the following day, they rose, marched the intervening distance, and silently descended upon the enemy.

The camp at Frenchtown was asleep, the drum roll just sounding reveille. This, surely, was the moment for attack, while the men were still in their blankets, but Procter went by the book, which insisted that an infantry charge be supported by cannon.

Precious moments slipped by, and the army's momentum slowed as Procter placed his pieces. A sharp-eyed Kentucky guard spotted the movement. A rifle exploded. The leading grenadier of the 41st dropped dead. A bullet had literally gone in one ear and out the other. Surprise was lost as the

The Battle of Frenchtown

battle began. Procter's caution would cost the lives of scores of good men.

It was still dark. The British and Canadians could see flashes of musket fire several hundred metres to the front but nothing else. Slowly, in the predawn murk a blurred line of figures took shape, standing out in front of the village. They fired a volley at this welcome target but the line stood fast. They fired again without effect. Who were these supermen who did not fall when the muskets roared? Dawn provided the answer. They had been aiming, not at their enemies, but at a line of wooden pickets that protected the village.

A second problem frustrated them. Procter had placed one of his three-pounders directly in front of his centre. The American fire – aimed at the gun – played upon the men behind it, while the gunners themselves were in the line of fire of their own men in their rear.

The fire grew hotter. Behind the palisades, the Americans could easily pick out targets against the lightening sky. When the British abandoned the three-pounder twenty yards (18 m) from the fence, the Kentuckians leaped over the fence and captured it. At that, a young British seaman seized the drag rope and hauled it back to the British line just as a musket ball shredded his heel.

Private Shadrach Byfield was fighting in Adam Muir's company of the 41st when the man on his left fell dead. It was light enough now to see the enemy and he spotted a Kentuckian coming through the palisades. "There's a man!" cried Byfield to a friend. "I'll have a shot at him." As he pulled the trigger, a ball struck him under the left ear. He toppled to the ground, cutting his friend's leg with his bayonet in the process.

Byfield was only twenty-three – a Wiltshire man who had joined the British army at eighteen. He was the third in his family to enlist, which had caused his poor mother to fall into a speechless fit from which she never recovered. Now he believed his last moment had come.

"Byfield is dead!" his friend cried out. Shadrach Byfield replied, in some wonder, "I believe I be." An age-old question flashed across his mind, a question that must occur to every soldier the instant he falls in battle. "Is this death?" he asked himself. *Is this how men die?*

But he wasn't dead. He raised his head and began to creep off on his hands and knees.

"Byfield," called a sergeant, "shall I take you to the doctor?"

But Shadrach Byfield, at twenty-three, was an old soldier. "Never mind me, go and help the men," he said and made his way to a barn to have his wounds dressed. There he encountered a sight so disturbing that he could never forget it – a young midshipman wounded in the knee, crying in pain for his mother, convinced he was going to die.

At the palisade, John Richardson felt as if he was sleepwalking. The early call and the six-mile (10 km) march had exhausted him. Even as the balls began to whistle above his head, he continued to feel drowsy. He tried to fire his musket but found it wouldn't respond. Someone the night before had stolen his flintlock and replaced it with a damaged part.

The infantry manual listed twelve separate drill movements for firing a Brown Bess musket and Richardson went through all of them without success. All he got was a flash in the pan. He found a bit of wire, tried to fix his weapon, fired again, got another flash. He felt more frustration and then fear at being fired on by an unseen foe and not being able to shoot back. Later he came to realize that he had fired fifty rounds and that not one had any effect on the pickets and probably not on the enemy either. The musket was a wretchedly inaccurate weapon.

To his horror, Richardson noted that the American sharpshooters were picking off the wounded British and Canadians as they tried to crawl to safety and some were making use of the tomahawk and scalping knife. He struggled valiantly with his useless weapon when he heard his name called. Somebody shouted that his brother had been wounded – young Robert's right leg was shattered as he applied a match to a gun. Now in great pain, Robert begged to be carried off, not to the staff section where his father was caring for the wounded, but to another part of the field so that he might escape his parent's wrath. And there, Shadrach Byfield witnessed his suffering.

On the left of the British line, Richardson could hear the war whoops of the Indians who, with the help of the Canadian militia, were driving directly through the open fields in which Lieutenant-Colonel Wells insisted on placing the regulars of the 17th U.S. Infantry. Wells was still at the Maumee. The second-in-command, Major McClanahan, could not hold his unprotected position. The troops retreated to the frozen river.

Now the Americans were in full flight across the river with Lieutenant-Colonel William Caldwell and a band of Indians under Roundhead, Split Log, and Walk-in the-Water in hot pursuit. One of the Wyandots overtook an American officer and was about to tomahawk him when Caldwell interceded, made him a prisoner, and took him to the rear. The Kentuckian, catching him off guard, drew his knife and slit Caldwell's throat from ear to ear. But the wound was shallow and Caldwell, who was as tough as his Indian followers, caught his attacker's arm, pulled the dagger from his throat and plunged it again and again into his prisoner's body until he was dead. Caldwell survived.

But where, when all this was going on, was the general? Winchester had awakened to the sound of musket fire and howitzer bombs exploding. He ran to the barn, borrowed a horse from his host, and dashed to action. His two battalion commanders, William Lewis and John Allen, joined him, and the three attempted to gather the fleeing men together under the bank of the Raisin. It was too late. The troops, pursued by the Indians, were in a panic. Lewis sent two companies to the right flank to reinforce the regulars, but these too were in retreat.

The three officers withdrew across the river and attempted a second rally behind the fences on the south side. It was hopeless. The men dashed past into a narrow lane leading to the main road. That was suicide, because the Indians were ahead of them and behind them on both sides of the lane. One hundred men were shot, tomahawked, and scalped. Winchester attempted a third rally in an orchard about a mile and a half (2.5 km) from the village. It also failed.

The right flank was now in full retreat, the men throwing away their weapons in panic. John Allen, shot in the thigh during his attempts to stall the retreat, limped on for two miles (3 km) until he could go no further. Exhausted and in pain, he slumped onto a log, resigned to his fate. One of the Potawatomi chiefs, seeing his officer's uniform, decided to capture and ransom him. But just as he showed his intention a second Indian moved in. Allen killed him with a swipe of his sword. The other shot the colonel dead and scalped him.

Winchester and Lewis were more fortunate. They fell into the hands of Roundhead, the principal chief of the Wyandot. Roundhead, after stripping the general of his cocked hat, coat, and epaulettes, took the two officers and Winchester's seventeen-year-old son by a roundabout route back behind the British lines. The battle for the village was still raging, but Winchester, noting Procter's artillery, dazed by the rout, and despairing of any reinforcements from Harrison, gave up hope. As the Indians returned, each with as many as eight or nine scalps hanging from his belt,

Winchester asked to see Procter. The British commander was blunt.

"Some of your troops, sir, are defending themselves from the fort in a state of desperation – had you not better surrender them?"

"I have no authority to do so," replied Winchester, shivering in his silk shirt. "My command has devolved upon the senior officer in the fort, as you are pleased to call it."

Procter warned that if there was no surrender he would have to set the town on fire. If he was forced to attack, he could not be responsible for the conduct of the Indians or the lives of the Americans. If Winchester would surrender he would be responsible for both. Winchester repeated that he was no longer in command but would recommend surrender to his people.

The command of the American force still fighting in the palisade had devolved on Major George Madison, a forty-nine-year-old veteran of the Revolution. At this moment he was concerned about the possession of an empty barn 150 yards (135 m) from the palisade. If the enemy seized that building, they would hold a commanding position overlooking the defenders. Madison called for a volunteer to set fire to the barn. A young ensign, William O. Butler, stepped forward, seized a blazing stick of firewood, vaulted the fence, and dashed toward the barn under direct fire from the British and Indians on both sides.

Butler reached the barn, flung the burning brand into a pile of hay, and raced back through a hail of musket balls.

*William Butler flings the burning brand.*

He had almost reached the safety of his own lines when he realized the hay had not caught. Back he went again, re-entered the barn, fanned the hay into a roaring blaze, and outran the Indians trying to head him off. With his clothes ripped by passing musket balls, he tumbled across the pickets and came to a full stop, standing upright trying to catch his breath. It was then that a musket ball struck him full in the chest. Fortunately, it had lost its force. Butler survived. Like his commander, George Madison, he would one day run for governor of Kentucky.

Now came a lull in the fighting. Of the sixteen British gunners, thirteen were casualties. The remainder were too numb with cold to fire their weapons. Their ammunition was low. Procter had withdrawn his forces into the woods, waiting for the Indians to return from the chase before resuming the attack. The defenders seized this interlude to devour some breakfast. That was the moment when Winchester agreed to attempt a surrender.

The Americans, seeing a flag of truce, thought that Procter was asking for time to bury his dead. It did not occur to any that surrender was being proposed. When he learned the truth, George Madison was mortified. And yet he knew his position was hopeless, for he had only a third of a keg of cartridges left. The reserve supply remained at the Navarre house across the river.

However, Madison insisted on conditions: "It has been customary for the Indians to massacre the wounded prisoners after a surrender," he reminded Procter. "I shall therefore not agree to any capitulation which General Winchester may direct, unless the safety and protection of all the prisoners shall be stipulated."

Procter stamped his foot:

"Sir, do *you* mean to dictate for *me?* "

"I mean to dictate for myself," Madison coolly replied. "We prefer to sell our lives as dearly as possible rather than be massacred in cold blood."

Procter agreed, but not in writing. Private property, he promised, would be respected. Sleighs would be sent the following morning for the American sick and wounded. The disabled would be protected by a proper guard.

Thus the battle ended. Some of the troops pleaded with their officers not to surrender, saying they would rather die in action. But the general feeling was one of despair. To Thomas P. Dudley, another Lexington volunteer, "the mortification of the thought of surrender, the Spartan band who fought like heroes, the tears shed, the wringing of hands, the swelling of hearts, indeed, the scene beggars description."

Only thirty-three men had managed to escape. McClanahan, Wells's second-in-command was one. Private John J. Brice was another. He got away by pulling off his shoes and running through the snow in his stocking feet in order to leave tracks resembling those of an Indian in moccasins. Thus he became the first man to report the defeat and surrender to Harrison.

Winchester's loss was appalling. Two hundred Kentuckians were dead or wounded. Another seven hundred were prisoners of the British. But the worst was yet to come. The blow to American morale, already bruised by the losses at Detroit and Queenston, was overwhelming. As for Harrison, the Battle of Frenchtown had already wrecked his plans. His left wing had been shattered. His advance on Detroit was halted indefinitely. He had to withdraw to the Maumee out of reach of the enemy. Largely because of the Indians, the idea of a swift victory over Canada was gone forever.

# CHAPTER SIX
## *Massacre*

I N FRENCHTOWN, ON January 23, young William Atherton woke at dawn to feel the wound in his shoulder
throbbing. He could not escape a feeling of dread that had
tormented his sleep. An ominous stillness had come over
the village where the American wounded were still held.
Procter, fearing an early attack from Harrison, had long
since dragged his own wounded off on sleds. Since there
were not enough of these for the Americans, he had promised to return early in the morning to take them all to
Amherstburg.

But the promise made no sense. If Procter was afraid of
Harrison, why would he then return for the wounded? If he
didn't fear him, why had he taken everybody with him
except one officer, Major Reynolds, and three interpreters?

Actually, Harrison, learning of the disaster, had withdrawn his relief force. In the course of the criticism that
followed, nobody bothered to ask why. With Procter's forces off balance and Fort Amherstburg virtually defenceless,
Harrison might easily have snatched victory from defeat.

But he contented himself with putting all the blame on Winchester.

The camp at Frenchtown was uneasy. Some time in the dark hours of the night, Reynolds and the interpreters had slipped away. Atherton's fears were further aroused by an Indian, apparently a chief, who spoke fluent English and came into his quarters the evening before, apparently trying to get information about Harrison's movements. But just as he left, the Indian made an oddly chilling remark: "I am afraid some of the mischievous boys will do some mischief before morning," he said.

The sun had been up for more than an hour when Atherton's fears were realized. Without warning the door of the house in which he and some of the wounded were being cared for was forced open. An Indian, his face smeared with red and black paint, appeared waving a tomahawk, followed by several others. Their purpose was loot. They began to strip the clothing and the blankets from the wounded men, groaning on the floor.

Atherton, near the door, managed to slip out of the room, only to come face to face with one of the most savage-looking Indians he had ever seen. His face was painted jet black. Half a bushel of feathers were fastened to his scalp lock. An immense tomahawk gleamed in his right hand. A scalping knife hung from his belt. He seized Atherton by the collar, propelled him out the front door, led him through the gate and down the river for a hundred yards (90 m) to the home of Jean-Baptiste Jerome, where several wounded officers had spent the night. The building had also done duty as a tavern, and the Indians were ransacking the cellars for whiskey.

In front of the house, Atherton saw a scarecrow figure, bleeding, barefoot, and clad only in a shirt and drawers. This was Captain Nathaniel Hart, commander of the Lexington Light Infantry, inspector of the Northwest Army. He was the messenger whom Harrison sent to Winchester the night before the battle. He was twenty-eight and wealthy, having made a fortune in hemp. Now he was pleading for his life.

The previous night, Hart, badly wounded in the knee, was visited by an old friend, a Canadian militia captain, William Elliott, who had once been cared for in the Hart home in Lexington during a bout of illness. Hart had Elliott's promise that he would send his personal sleigh for him in the morning and bring him back to Amherstburg. In fact Elliott had assured all the wounded and injured in Jerome's house that they were in no danger. That promise was hollow. They were all in deadly peril. Some were already dying under the tomahawk blows of the Indians.

Hart turned to an Indian he recognized – the same English-speaking chief who Atherton had encountered the evening before. He reminded him of Elliott's promise.

"Elliott has deceived you, he does not intend to fulfil his promise," the Indian replied.

"If you will agree to take me, I'll give you a horse or a hundred dollars," Hart declared. "You shall have it on our arrival at Malden."

"I cannot take you."

"Why?"

"You are too badly wounded."

"Then", asked Captain Hart, "what do you intend to do with us?"

"Boys," said the Indian, "you are all to be killed."

Hart kept his composure and said a brief prayer. Atherton expected at any moment to feel the blow of a tomahawk. A scene of pure horror followed. Captain Paschal Hickman emerged from Jerome's house, dragged by an Indian who threw him face down into the snow. Hickman had already been tomahawked. He died as Atherton watched in terror. Then, taking advantage of the confusion, Atherton began to edge away slowly, hoping not to be seen.

Albert Ammerman, another unwilling witness, crouched on a log, guarded by his Indian captor. A private in the 1st Regiment of Kentucky Volunteers, he had been wounded in the thigh but had been doing his best to conceal his injury, for he knew it was the Indians' practice to kill all who could not walk. He watched helplessly while the Indians looted the houses, stripped the clothes from the wounded, tomahawked and scalped their prey, and set fire to the buildings. Some, still alive, forced their heads out of the windows, half-enveloped in smoke and flames, seeking rescue. But there was no rescue.

72

Ammerman was marched off at last toward Brownstown with some other prisoners. After limping about half a mile (0.8 km), they were overtaken. One Indian had Captain Hart in custody and was having a violent argument with another, apparently over the reward that Hart had offered for their safe conduct. As Ammerman watched, the two took aim at each as if to end the quarrel. But they did not fire. Instead they turned upon their prisoner, pulled him from his horse, knocked him down with a war club, tomahawked him, scalped him, stripped him of his remaining clothes, money and belongings.

Ammerman, who was later ransomed in Detroit, noted that Hart during these final moments refrained from making any pleas. He appeared to the end to be perfectly calm. The news of his death, when it finally reached Lexington three months later, would cause a particular shiver of despair and fury in Kentucky. For this mangled and naked corpse, thrown like carrion onto the side of the road, was once the brother-in-law of Henry Clay, a famous American politician.

Back at Frenchtown, little William Atherton – he was only five foot five (1.65 m) – was trying to reach a small log building some distance from the scene of horror. He edged toward it and was a few steps from it when a Potawatomi seized him and asked where he was wounded. Atherton placed his hand on his shoulder. The Indian felt it and found it was not serious. He decided that Atherton would be his prize for later ransom. He wrapped him in a blanket,

*The slaughter of the prisoners at Frenchtown*

gave him a hat, took him to the back door of one of the houses and put him in charge of all his plunder.

Atherton was flabbergasted. For the best part of an hour he had expected certain death. Now he lived in the faint hope that his life might be spared. He experienced "one of those sudden transitions of mind impossible to either conceive or express, except by those whose unhappy lot it has been, to be placed in like circumstances."

As the house blazed behind him, Atherton watched his fellow prisoners being dragged away to Brownstown. For the first time perhaps, he had been aware of the value a man places on his own life. He saw members of his own company, old acquaintances, so badly wounded they could hardly be moved from their beds, suddenly leap up, hearing that the Indians would tomahawk all who could not leave on foot. They hobbled past him on sticks. Unable to keep up, they were soon butchered.

After two hours, Atherton's captor returned with an army pack horse and a great deal of plunder. The Potawatomi handed his prisoner the bridle and the two set off on the road to Brownstown, bordered now by a ghastly hedgerow of mutilated corpses.

They halted for the night at Sandy Creek, where a number of Potawatomi were encamped. Here, around a roaring fire of fence rails, the Indians fed their captives gruel. And here another grisly scene took place. An Indian walked up to Private Charles Searls and proposed to exchange his moccasins for the soldier's shoes. Following the exchange a brief conversation took place with the Indian asking how many men Harrison had with him. Suddenly the name of the Hero of Tippecanoe drove him into a sudden rage. With his anger rising, he called Searls a "Madison", raised his tomahawk, and struck him a deep blow on the shoulder. Searls, bleeding profusely, clutched the weapon embedded in his flesh and tried to resist. A surgeon's mate, Gustavus Bower, told him his fate was inevitable. Searls closed his eyes as the fatal blow fell. Not long after that, three more men were murdered at random.

When Atherton asked his captor if the Indians intended to kill all the prisoners, the Indian nodded. Atherton tried to eat, but he had no stomach for it even though he had had little food for three days. Then he realized his captor didn't understand English, and so a vestige of hope returned.

The march resumed with many alarms. Atherton was in daily fear of his life. He slept with a kerchief tied around his neck in the belief that the Indians would want to steal it before tomahawking him in his sleep, thus giving him some warning. But they did not kill him. His captor, whose brother had been been killed at the River Raisin, had other plans.

It was the custom of the Potawatomi, among others, to adopt healthy captives into the families of those who had lost sons in the same engagement. It was some time before Atherton realized that his enemies did not intend to kill or ransom him. On the contrary, they were determined to turn him into an Indian and almost succeeded.

Dr. John Todd, a surgeon with the Kentucky Volunteers, was taken to the British camp where he again met Captain William Elliott. He urged Elliott to send a sleigh back to pick up some of the badly wounded, but Elliott knew it was too late and said so. When Todd pressed his case, Elliott said that charity began at home, and that the British and Canadians must be cared for first. He added, in some exasperation, that it was impossible to restrain the Indians and tried to explain that they were simply seeking revenge for their own losses. The Battle of Tippecanoe was only fourteen months in the past, the attacks along the Mississinewa less than two.

Along the frozen shores of the River Raisin a great stillness fell. The cold was numbing. Nothing moved. Those settlers who still remained in Frenchtown did not venture outside their doors.

In the little orchard across the river, along the narrow lane that led from the Navarre home and beside the Detroit River road, the bodies of the Americans lay, unburied. The Potawatomi had made it known that any white man who dared to touch the remains of the any of the hated Harrison men would meet a similar fate.

The naked corpses lay strewn for many kilometres along the roadside in the grotesque attitude of men who, in a sudden flash, realize their last moment had come.

There, contorted in death, lay the flower of Kentucky: Captain Hart and Captain Hickman, Lieutenant-Colonel John Allen and Captain John Wollfolk, Winchester's aide-de-camp, who once offered a thousand dollars to anybody who would purchase him, but was tomahawked in spite of it. There was Captain John Simpson, a congressman, and Ensign Levi Wells, the son of Lieutenant-Colonel Sam Wells of the 4th Infantry, and Allen Darnell, whose brother looked on helplessly as he was scalped because he could not keep up with the others, and Ebenezer Blythe, a surgeon's mate, tomahawked in the act of offering ransom. And there, like a discarded doll, was the body of young Captain Price of the Jessamine Blues whose last letter home gave instructions for the upbringing of his two-year-old son.

The war which had begun so gently turned ugly as all wars must. The mannerly days were over. New emotions – hatred, fury, a thirst for revenge, a nagging sense of guilt – distorted the tempers of the neighbours who once lived peacefully on both sides of the embattled border. And it was not over. Peace was still two years away. The blood had only begun to flow.

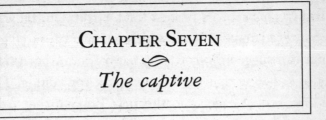

# CHAPTER SEVEN

## The captive

IN APRIL 1813, little William Atherton was still a captive of the Potawatomi in Michigan Territory. To him, home seemed to be on another planet.

Adopted into a Potawatomi family to replace a son killed at Frenchtown, he now lived as an Indian, wore Indian buckskin, observed Indian customs. He hunted with bow and arrow, danced the corn dance, slept in a wigwam, ate boiled corn and bristly hog meat. He neither heard nor spoke English.

His only contact with white civilization was a tattered Lexington newspaper found among the Indians' effects. That was his sole comfort. He read and re-read it, clinging to the brittle pages as a reminder that somewhere beyond the brooding, snow-covered forests, there was really another world – a world that he once took for granted, but which came back to him now as if in a dream. Would he ever see it again? As winter gave way to spring, Atherton gave way to despair, stealing out of camp for moments of solitude when he could think of home and weep without being discovered.

In May, his captors headed for Detroit. On the way, they encountered another band which had just captured a young American surgeon in battle. What battle? Atherton had no way of knowing that the war was still continuing. The two men conversed eagerly in the first English that Atherton had heard in three months. Then the other departed, Atherton believed to his death.

They reached Amherstburg but Atherton had no hope of escape. With his long, swarthy face and his matted brown hair, uncut for months, he was just another Indian to the British, who failed to notice his blue eyes. When the band moved across to Spring Wells, to draw rations at the British commissary, Atherton's Indian father learned, with delight, that his new son could write. He had him double the original number of family members on the chit, thus increasing the handout of provisions. Again, the British did not realize that Atherton was white.

He lost track of time. Crawling with vermin, half-starved, with no hope of escape from the family that nurtured but also guarded him, he threw himself on their mercy and pleaded to be ransomed. To his surprise, his Indian father agreed, though reluctantly. It was clear that Atherton had become part of the family, more a son than a captive. They could not refuse him, even though it meant losing him.

*William Atherton's only contact with white civilization was a tattered Lexington newspaper.*

Eventually, in Detroit, they found a man who would give a pony for him. Atherton bid his Indian parents goodbye – not without sorrow, for they had, in their own fashion, been kind – and became a prisoner of war. All that summer he was lodged in a British guardhouse, almost naked, sleeping on the floor with a log for a pillow, wondering about the course of the war.

And the war went on. Of the triumphs and defeats of his own people, Atherton knew nothing. Only when his captors returned from the unsuccessful British siege at Fort Stevenson at Lower Sandusky, their faces peppered with small shot, did he have an inkling that beyond the quarter-house walls, all along the border men were still fighting and dying.

Summer gave way to fall. On September 10, 1813, Atherton and his fellow prisoners could hear the rumble of heavy guns across Lake Erie and knew that a naval battle was raging. At last, a private soldier whispered the truth: the Americans had defeated the British fleet and Erie had become an American lake. The victory touched off a major retreat. The British packed up hastily in the face of a new advancing army under Harrison. Atherton could hardly wait for the Kentucky forces to arrive and free him. But that was not to be. The prisoners were hurried across to the Canadian shore and herded up the Thames Valley, on to York, Kingston, and Montreal.

It seemed as if the entire city of Montreal turned out to stare at them – verminous, shaggy, half-starved after a journey of nine hundred miles (1,400 km). As Atherton trudged down the cobbled streets he noticed the doors and windows crammed with curious women. In the jail they were given a little "Yankee beef," taunted with the fact that it had been purchased by the British from Americans trading with the enemy.

Two weeks later they were sent on to Quebec city. The Kentuckians' reputation had preceded them. The Quebeckers thought of them as wild men – savage forest creatures, half-human, half-beast. They crowded to the jail, peering at the captives as they would at animals in a zoo, astonished, even disappointed, to find they did not live up to their billing. One man gazed at them for several minutes, then delivered the general verdict: "Why, they look just like other people."

Beyond the prison the war raged on. Eventually Atherton was released and sent back across the border. In Pittsburgh he met a group of vaguely familiar men – British prisoners of war. Who were they? Where had he seen them before? Then he remembered. These were soldiers who were once his guards when he was a captive in Detroit. It all seemed a long time ago.

Atherton's story was not unique. Eighty or ninety Kentuckians were captured by the Potawatomi braves, and of these a good number were adopted into Indian families. Timothy Mallory had all his hair shaved off except for a scalp lock, his face painted half-black, half-red, his ears pierced for rings. John Davenport was painted, adorned with earrings, bracelets and a silver band wound round his shaved skull.

"We make an Indian out of you," one of his captors promised, and "by'n by you have squaw, by'n by you have a gun and horse and go hunting."

Both these men lived as Indians for several months. Like Atherton, who preferred his treatment by Indians to that of the British (he found them "brave, generous, hospitable, kind and . . . honest"), they were surprised to discover that their Indian families were generally fond of them. The women went out of their way to protect them when the braves indulged in drinking bouts. When at last they were ransomed, the Indians were clearly reluctant to part with them.

No one to this day knows exactly how many Kentucky Volunteers were held captive by the natives, adopted into families that had lost sons in battle. No one knows exactly how many escaped or were ransomed. But it is possible, even probable, that as the war rolled on, there were still some Kentuckians who went entirely native, took Indian wives, and removed themselves from white society.

There was irony in this. But then it was a war of irony and paradox – a war fought over a cause that was removed before the fighting began; a war that everyone claimed to have won – except the real victors, who, being Indians, were really losers, a war designed to seize by force a nation that could have been attacked by stealth.

And were there in the forests of Michigan among the Potawatomi – those veterans of Tippecanoe – certain warriors of lighter skin and alien background? If so, that was the final irony. Ever since the days of Thomas Jefferson, it had been official American policy to try to turn the Indians into white men. Who can blame the Indians if, in their last, desperate, doomed resistance, they should manage in some measure to turn the tables?

# Index

ALLEN, LIEUTENANT-COLONEL
    JOHN, 46, 49, 62, 63, 77
American Revolution, 10, 32, 66
Amherstburg, 9, 40, 51, 56, 69,
    71, 80
Ammerman, Albert, 72–73
Askin, John, 9, 10
Atherton, William, 54–55,
    69–78, 79–84

BATTLE CONDITIONS:
    alcohol, 17–18;
    disease, 17, 35, 37;
    shortage of weapons and pro-
        visions, 32–33, 35, 37–38,
        42, 66
Black Bird, 42
Blythe, Ebenezer, 78
Bonaparte, Napoleon, 12
Bower, Gustavus, 76
Brice, Private John J., 68
Brownstown, 57, 73, 75

Butler, William O., 64–66
Byfield, Private Shadrach, 59–60,
    61

CALDWELL, LIEUTENANT-
    COLONEL WILLIAM, 62
Campbell, Lieutenant-Colonel
    John, 36
Canada:
    American immigration to,
        10–11;
    and causes of war, 11–12;
    new feelings of nationalism, 19
Clay, Henry, 73
Combs, Leslie, 47

DARNELL, ALLEN, 78
Darnell, Elias, 49
Davenport, John, 83–84
Detroit, 10, 30, 32, 35, 36, 40, 46,
    51, 56, 68, 80, 82, 83
Dudley, Thomas P., 67

EDWARDS, NINIAN, 42
Elkheart River, 33
Elliott, Captain William, 71, 77

FORT AMHERSTBURG, see
   Amherstburg
Fort Detroit, see Detroit
Fort Harrison, 25
Fort McArthur, 47
Fort Stevenson, 82
Fort Wayne, 41
Fort Winchester, 33
France, 12
Frenchtown, 43–45, 46, 48, 49,
   50, 51–53, 57–68, 69, 70, 73,
   77, 79;
   Battle of Frenchtown, 15,
      50–68, 79
   massacre, 69–78

GEORGE III, 56
Great Britain:
   and alliance with Indians, 13–
      14, 20, 27, 29, 40–41, 42–43;
   and causes of war, 11, 12

HARRISON, WILLIAM HENRY,
   20–21, 25–29, 30, 32–36, 38,
   40, 41, 42–43, 44, 46–48, 49,
   53–54, 57, 67, 68, 69–70, 71,
   76, 82;
   and attempted purchase of
      native hunting grounds,
      20–25, 27;
   and scorched earth policy, 33,
      41–43
Hart, Captain Nathaniel, 71–73,
   77

Hickman, Captain Paschal, 72,
   77

ILLINOIS TERRITORY, 35, 42
Indiana territory, 20, 33, 35, 43
Indians:
   allegiance to British, 13–14,
      19, 29, 30, 40–41;
   and Battle of Tippecanoe,
      25–29, 57, 76, 77;
   casualties and damages suf-
      fered 26–27, 33, 41–42;
   desire for revenge, 27–29,
      41–42, 77, 85;
   and Harrison's attempt to pur-
      chase land, 20–25, 27;
   numbers of, 14, 29, 38, 40, 43,
      57;
   practice of taking prisoners,
      70–78, 79–85;
   reputation of, 14, 32, 40–41,
      66–67;
   strategic importance of in the
      war, 13–14, 20, 30, 61–62,
      68;
   Algonquin, 9;
   Choctaw, 41;
   Creek, 41;
   Delaware, 21;
   Eel, 21;
   Miami, 21, 36, 43, 57;
   Mohawk, 14, 30, 35;
   Ottawa, 9, 43;
   Potawatomi, 21, 42, 43, 57, 63,
      73, 75, 76, 77, 84, 85;
   Shawnee, 20, 21;
   Wabash, 41;

Wyandot, 57, 62, 63

JEFFERSON, THOMAS, 12–13, 19, 85

Jerome, Jean-Baptiste, 71

Judy, Captain, 42

KINGSTON, 82

LAKE ERIE, AMERICAN CONTROL OF, 82

Lewis, Lieutenant-Colonel William, 49, 50, 54, 62, 63

Looting and vandalism, 27, 33, 70–71, 72

Lower Canada, 13

MADISON, JAMES, 21

Madison, Major George, 64, 66–67, 76

Mallory, Timothy, 83

Maumee River rapids, 33–34, 36, 40, 42, 43, 44, 47–48, 49, 54, 62, 68

McClanahan, Major, 62, 67

Michigan territory, 30, 35, 43, 79

Mississinewa, 36, 57, 77

Montreal, 82–83

Muir, Adam, 60

NAVARRE, COLONEL FRANCIS, 52, 77

Navarre, Peter, 52, 54

Norton, William, 30

PITTSBURGH, 83

Presqu'Isle, 49–50

Price, Colonel James, 50, 78

Prisoners, 9–10, 30, 68, 70–78, 79–85

Procter, Lieutenant-Colonel Henry, 40, 42, 43, 56–59, 64, 66–67, 69

"The Prophet," 23, 25, 29, 41

Prophet's Town, 23, 25, 27, 29, 32

QUEBEC CITY, 83

Queen Charlotte, 56

Queenston Heights, Battle of, 30, 35, 36, 68

REYNOLDS, MAJOR EBENEZER, 43, 44, 69, 70

Richardson, John, 9–10, 14–15, 57, 60–61

Richardson, Robert, 57, 61

River Raisin, 43, 49, 51, 56, 76, 77

Rocky River, 57

Roundhead, Chief, 57, 62, 63

SANDY CREEK, 75

Scott, Colonel John, 33

Searls, Private Charles, 75–76

Shelby, Isaac, 35

Simpson, Captain John, 78

Split Log, 62

Spring Wells, 80

St. George, Lieutenant-Colonel, 56

TECUMSEH, 14, 20–25, 29, 30, 36, 38, 41, 42;
and Indian confederacy, 23, 41

Tippecanoe, Battle of, 25–29, 32, 57, 76, 77

Todd, Dr. John, 77

Tories, see United Empire Loyalists

Trafalgar, Battle of, 12
Troops, American:
  casualties, 36, 37, 63, 68, 77;
  4th U.S. Infantry, 26, 78;
  Jessamine Blues, 50, 78;
  Kentucky Volunteers, 32, 41,
    49, 50, 58, 59, 72, 77, 82, 83,
    84;
  Lexington Light Infantry, 71;
  militia, 18–19;
  morale, 18–19, 32, 36, 37, 46,
    50, 52, 53, 67, 68;
  motives for fighting, 12, 32
  numbers of, 13, 25, 26, 32, 35,
    36, 37;
  Ohio Volunteers, 41–42;
  17th U.S. Infantry, 62;
  shortage of weapons and pro-
    visions, 32–33, 35, 36,
    37–38, 45
Troops, British:
  casualties, 66;
  41st regiment, 9, 58, 60;
  numbers of, 13, 40, 57;
  Provincial Marine, 57;
  regular army, 13, 14;
  Royal Navy, 12;
  shortage of weapons and pro-
    visions, 42, 66
Troops, Canadian militia, 10, 18,
  36, 43, 62;
  Canadian Voltigeurs, 18;
  Essex militia, 43;
  Glengarry Fencibles, 18;

Incoporated Militia of Upper
  Canada, 18;
  motives for fighting, 9, 11–12,
    18
  Sedentary Militia, 18;
  Select Embodied Militia, 18

UNITED EMPIRE LOYALISTS, 10
United States:
  attitude toward Indians, 14;
  and causes of war, 12
Upper Canada, 13

WALK-IN-THE-WATER, 62
War of 1812:
  causes of, 11, 12;
  declaration of, 12, 30
Water routes, control of, 13, 82
Waterloo, Battle of, 12
Weapons:
  "Brown Bess", 14–15, 61;
  Tennessee rifle, 15;
  cannons, 15–17, 50;
  bombs, 17
Wells, Ensign Levi, 78
Wells, Lieutenant-Colonel
  Samuel, 52, 53, 62, 78
Winchester, General James, 37,
  39, 40, 43, 44–45, 46, 47–48,
  49, 51, 52–54, 62, 63–64, 66,
  67, 68, 70, 71
Windsor, 9
Wollfolk, Captain John, 77–78

YORK, 82

*Coming Soon*

Book No. 4

# CANADA UNDER SIEGE

The Americans seize Little York (Toronto) and burn the
Parliament Buildings.

A young boy leads the Canadians to win the Battle of
Stoney Creek.

Laura Secord warns the British of the Battle of
Beaver Dams.

James FitzGibbon's "Bloody Boys" hit Black Rock.

*Stories of traitors, heroes, guerrilla fighters, turncoats,
villains, and doomed generals in the next instalment of*
**The Battles of the War of 1812**